I0474330

How To Write Your Marketing Plan

P A Flanagan

Copyright © 2012 P A Flanagan

All rights reserved.

ISBN: 1469985578
ISBN-13: 978-1469985572

CONTENTS

1 Introduction to Using this Guide

A marketing plan provides direction for your marketing activities. One way to think about your marketing plan is as a road map, with detailed directions on how to get to your destination. When your marketing plan is carefully researched, thoughtfully considered and evaluated, it will help your organization achieve its goals.

The marketing plan details what you want to accomplish with your marketing strategy and how you will measure your performance against your objectives.

This marketing framework gives you a structured approach to producing your own marketing plan. This guide follows the logical stages of the marketing planning process.

A marketing plan typically includes these chapters:

- Executive Summary
- Business Mission
- External Marketing Audit
- Internal Marketing Audit
- SWOT analysis & Assumptions
- Marketing Objectives
- Core Strategy
- Marketing Mix Decisions
- Organization and Implementation
- Control

The following sections of this guide will introduce each chapter of the marketing plan, along with a sample marketing plan for Childcare.com.

Childcare.com is a fictitious new online business startup.

2 Executive Summary

The Executive Summary describes the report's major findings and recommendations. The objective is to provide the busy reader with the major issues contained in your marketing plan.

The Executive Summary allows the reader to gain insight to key outcomes without having to read all of the report. Bullet points can be used to present the key points in your Executive Summary.

The Executive Summary should be completed last, once you have finished all other sections of the Marketing Plan.

Childcare.com Sample

Mary Bloggs and Joe Bloggs are the company founders and business promoters. We are passionate about technology. We believe that it can enhance the way we do things in a faster and more effective way, leaving us more time to spend on the things that are important to us.

As a busy family we have used many forms of childcare over the years, from using online au pair agencies to recruit ourselves, as well as crèches, after school clubs and numerous camps and activities for our children. We are now marrying our experiences as childcare consumers with our passion for technology to develop Childcare.com.

Childcare.com is a destination where parents can source solutions from everything from domestic childcare to after school care.

Unlike other online services we provide targeted recommendations, along with the ability to answer as many care seeker questions there and then. Our initial product focuses on domestic homecare, namely nannies, au pairs, babysitters and child minders.

The rapid increase of mothers in the workforce over the last forty years has produced high demand for all types of childcare. More than ever before, consumers have a growing appetite for gathering information prior to making a decision to use a service or to purchase goods. The internet has made information more widely available. Consumers of childcare are now better informed about childcare and its impact on all areas of child development.

Traffic volume analysis on the monthly visits to online agencies, such as care.com, clearly demonstrates there is a demand for online resources helping families to source their own childcare providers. Care.com receives in access of 4m visits per month.

Childcare.com phase 1 launches with the service offering for care seekers (families) to advertise and recruit care providers (au pairs, nannies, childminders) directly. The marketing strategy is to penetrate the market and gradually gain market share by effectively implementing an expansion plan. Subsequent phases of Childcare.com will adopt a growth strategy of implementing new related services for existing markets.

Our unique selling point will focus on how Childcare.com is here to help families find childcare that meets their needs. Childcare.com takes the pain out of recruiting carers.

Childcare.com is a mid-range service offering.

To be a successful childcare resource, it is essential to have a healthy database of childcare providers, both formal and informal, matching the requirements of care seekers. Both push and pull marketing strategies will be utilized to drive traffic to the website. As Childcare.com is an online business, search engine optimization (SEO) and digital marketing will be used to target all three customer segments (care seekers, care providers and business advertisers). Initially, Childcare.com will be marketed to the English speaking countries— the UK, the USA and Australia, including expats living abroad. Following is a summary of the childcare market within each target country.

- UK – In 2009 the childcare market was valued at £4.1 billion.

- Australia - In 2008, 1.5 million Australian children 12 years and younger had regular childcare arrangements.

- USA - Most U.S. children under five spend time on a regular basis each week in non-parental care. Regulated childcare centers increased from approximately 86,000 in 1991 to over 116,000 in 2003.

Mary Bloggs joins the management team as Managing Director/ Business Development. Mary brings her considerable experience and successful track record in project and operations management. As the Managing Director she will ensure that development and implementation of Childcare.com is delivered on time.

Joe Bloggs joins the management team as IT Director/ Lead Developer. Joe has over twelve years' experience in Information Technology including a degree in computer engineering. He is a Microsoft Certified Database Administrator, Sun Certified and Advanced Java Programmer.

As the main marketing activities are predominantly focused online, digital marketing experts will be employed to build up our marketing team. A paid advertising campaign on Google will support our digital marketing activities. Revenue from sales will support our paid advertising campaign, as well as the marketing resource procurement.

Our marketing systems will constantly track and monitor our website performance against our targets to ensure our strategy is effective.

3 Business Mission

The Business Mission is a broadly defined statement of purpose that distinguishes your business from others of the same type. Your mission could state 'What business your company is in?' and 'What business does it want to be in?' It may include the markets your business serves, the customer needs being satisfied, and the technology used.

A mission statement can dramatically affect the range of a firm's marketing activities by narrowing or broadening the competitive playing field.

For example, Childcare.com might define their business mission as;

Our mission is to be the number one online family resource, initially in the UK and gradually gaining market share within the USA and Australia.

Some good examples of mission statements are:

McDonald's *vision is to be the world's best quick service restaurant experience. Being the best means providing outstanding quality, service, cleanliness, and value, so that we make every customer in every restaurant smile.*

Google's *mission is to organize the world's information and make it universally accessible and useful.*

4 External Marketing Audit

A marketing audit is a systematic examination of the business marketing environment, objectives, strategies and activities, with a view to identifying key strategic issues, problem areas, and opportunities. It provides the basis upon which a plan of action to improve marketing performance can be built.

The external marketing audit focuses on:

Macro-environment – the macro-environment consists of broad environmental issues that impinge on your business, for example, what Economic, Socio-Cultural, Technological, Political/Legal, Ecological factors might impact your organization now and in the future?.

The Market – typically looks at the market your company operates in. What is your analysis of market size, growth rates and trends? The market is also a review of your customer analysis (who are they, what choice criteria do they use, how they rate competitive offerings and how is the market segmented.)

In the example below, Childcare.com used population census information, and government publications to gain an understanding of the potential size of the childcare market within their target countries.

Competition – competitor analysis typically examines who are your competitors, as well as answering key questions about them. What are their objectives and strategies? Strengths and weaknesses? Market share? Size and profitability?

Childcare.com Sample

Macro-environment

A table is a good way to display the results of your macro-environment analysis. The key areas to comment on are;

- Description of the issue identified
- Observations on potential impact
- Impact timescale
- Implications and importance

The table below summarizes the macro-environmental analysis for Childcare.com. You can easily adopt this table for your own macro-environmental analysis.

Description	Observations on potential impact	Impact Timescale	Implication and importance Impact Urgency
	H- High M – Medium L – Low	0-3 mths 6-9 mths 9-18 mths 18mths+	> increasing Critical <> undecided Important < decreasing Unimportant ? unsure Unsure
POLITICAL			
Policies to encourage training in the childcare industry are being implemented	M – higher quality care worker	18mths+	<> maybe opportunities to form partnerships with training organizations (affiliate programmes)
Policies to attract more men to childcare	M –more workers / higher salary & better terms of employment	18mths+	Develop website and logo with male care worker in mind
New childminding regulations	M –may result in less people working as childminders	18mths+	this may increase demand for alternative home-based childcare (au pairs, nannies)
Youth mobility programme in EU to encourage youth to travel abroad for work	M – greater number of youths willing to look for opportunities abroad	6-9 mths	> increasing numbers of university graduates seeking au pair nanny work abroad
ECONOMIC			
Higher unemployment	M – increased number of people seeking alternative work – i.e. childcare	0-3 mths	> numbers of carers seeking work
Large increase in associations and	H – greater number of	0-3 mths	> develop website to offer an advertising service for

businesses providing products, training, and other support to child care businesses.	associated businesses advertising their services		business promoters.
Reduced salaries/ longer hours/ family budget stretched	M – families looking for affordable / flexible childcare	0-3 mths	> numbers of families seeking more affordable childcare solutions – i.e. aupairs
SOCIAL			
Internet accepted source for online research	H – sites with good quality information in demand	0-3 mths	> online users have high expectations – good quality data/ online community / forums
Internet accepted medium for recruitment	H – demand for good recruitment sites	0-3 mths	> need good database for matching care seekers to care providers
TECHNOLOGICAL			
Demand for enhanced technology – mobile, faster internet speeds	H – internet users are more sophisticated and demand faster, better services	6-9 mths	> need to constantly review technology platform and refresh often
LEGAL			
No legal observations identified			Need to keep up to date with legal changes in the target markets

The Market

The market consists of an analysis on the following areas where applicable to your business:

- analyses of market size, growth rates and trends;

- your customer analysis including who they are, what choice criteria they use, how they rate competitive offerings and how the market is segmented.

- distribution analysis, which covers significant movements in powerbases, channel attractiveness analyses, physical distribution analyses and analysis of the role and interests of decision-makers and influences with distributor organizations.

Childcare.com Sample

Initially, marketing activities will focus on the UK, the USA and Australia. The key to success for a childcare solutions website is having a sufficient number of attractive childcare providers for each target location.

Marketing and promotion activities will target major cities to build up a healthy database of care givers and care seekers. The following sections provide some high level statistics on the childcare market within each target country.

United Kingdom

Laing and Buisson's Children's Nurseries and UK Market report for 2009 values the childcare market at £4.1 billion.[1]

The Children's Workforce Strategy published by the government estimated head count of the paid children's ECEC (birth to school age) workforce in England to be in the region of 683,000.

This is broken down into the following sectors. [2] The workforce is obviously greater when care for school age children is taken into account.

Private Sector	Headcount
Childcare/early years	204,800
Nannies	100,000
Education	76,200
Sports & Leisure	285,100

In 2009, there were 60,900 English home-based childminders registered with OFSTED. There are approximately 200,000 private pre-school childcare providers in the UK. The recruitment rates across the various types of ECEC settings in 2007 varied from 20% in nursery schools to 38% in full day care settings. The ECEC workforce is overwhelmingly female with less than 2% of employees being male.[3]

---

[1] http://www.daycaretrust.org.uk/data/files/Policy/childcare_and_the_recession__summary.pdf

[2] http://www.nscap.org.uk/doc/childrens%20workforce%20strategy.pdf

[3] http://www.tuc.org.uk/extras/raisingthebar.pdf

Australia

- In 2008, 1.5 million Australian children aged 12 years or less had regular childcare arrangements.
- Around 750,000 children usually attended formal childcare and about one million children attended some type of informal care (grandparents (19%), nannies & babysitters (10%)).
- Around 250,000 children attended both formal care and informal care.
- About two million children had no usual child care arrangements. Since 1999, there has been a trend towards an increased use of formal care. [4]

There were approximately 600,000 families in Australia in 2009 using non-parental childcare services[5]

All-day care is provided by a network of individuals (caregivers) who provide care in their own homes for other people's children. Based on the Australian Government Census of Child Care Services, IBISWorld estimates that in 2011-12 there will be about 110,000 children in family day care (childminders).[6]

USA

The USA population is estimated at 313,232,044, with 20% aged under 14 Years. Some statistics gathered from the UpJohn institute on childcare report[7];

---

[4] http://www.abs.gov.au/AUSSTATS/abs@.nsf/Lookup/4102.0Main+Features50Jun+2010

[5] http://www.mychild.gov.au/documents/docs/StateChildCareAus.pdf

[6] http://www.ibisworld.com.au/industry/default.aspx?indid=626

[7] http://research.upjohn.org/cgi/viewcontent.cgi?article=1012&context=up_bookchapters&sei-redir=1#search=%22childcare%20market%20size%20usa%22

Most U.S. children under five spend time on a regular basis each week in non-parental care.

Service type	Proportion of Children
Child care centres	28%
Home-based child care	14%
Other parent	27%
Relatives, friends	27%
Nanny, babysitter	4%

Regulated childcare centres increased from approximately 86,000 in 1991 to over 116,000 in 2003.

The unregulated market, the size of which is unknown, also continues to play an important role in the industry.

According to the Centres for the Child Care Workforce and the Human Services Policy Centre (2002), of the 2.3 million individuals paid to care for children ages 0–5 in the United States in a given week, approximately 550,000 adults are working in centre-based settings.

Target Customers

The main target customers for Childcare.com can be segmented into the following categories;

Home Decision Maker

The primary target market is the home decision maker (mostly mum, sometimes dad). They play the role of the family hub in communication and organizing the family. Mainly female who fall within the age group 30–45. She may work outside the home either on a full-time or part-time basis.

She is confident and well educated. Simplicity and clarity drives her – she's attracted to what's obvious, intuitive and incredibly easy to find, compare and buy. Instant quotes, the ability to customize, hassle free operations and fast delivery are paramount. Trust and ease are key.

Caregivers

Caregivers or care providers offer childcare services. They are either individuals (au pairs, nannies, babysitters) or businesses (child minders, day care).

Business Promoters

Businesses providing relevant services to the childcare market, for example, agencies, training schools, background checks, visa processing etc.

Market Trends

More than ever before, customers have a growing appetite for gathering information before making a decision to use a service or to purchase goods. Information is now more widely available, the internet being one of the main sources. In its survey on parents in 2004, the Daycare Trust (a UK-based childcare charity) reported that parents would like more information about the type of childcare available to them.

A major issue for parents was in trusting the service.

Consumers of childcare are now better informed about childcare and about its impact on all aspects of child development. The informed consumer is taking control of the way he/she learns and hears about products and services.

A key trend in the last 10 to 15 years has been the shift from parental care or informal childcare arrangements to formal childcare of young children aged 0-3 years.[8]

Investing in the childcare worker is also a major trend in many countries, as is the introduction of policies to attract more male workers to the sector.

Accompanying the growth of services in childcare has been a large increase in associations and businesses providing products, training, and other support to child care businesses.

---

[8]

http://www.eurofound.europa.eu/emcc/content/source/eu06016a.htm?p1=sectorfutures&p2=eu06015a&p3=Childcare_services

Competition

Competitor analysis typically examines the following areas:

- Who are the competitors to your company (actual and potential)?

- What are their objectives and strategies, strengths and weaknesses, market share, size and profitability?

- Are there any entry barriers that make market entry from new competitors difficult? These should be identified and listed if applicable to your company.

Childcare.com Sample

Care seekers may use the following services to find childcare;

Service	Overview	cost
Agency	Agency will recruit candidate on behalf of care seeker, for a fee.	Varies
Online agency	Provide online recruitment for families. For example, greataupair.com	Varies depending on service
Job sites that include care wanted jobs	Post job to generic job listing.	Costs vary
Free job postings	Post job on free sites like Craigslist	Free

The table below summarizes the research conducted into the traffic volumes and revenue streams of competitors.

Website	Based	Monthly Visitors *	Revenue Stream
Care.com	USA only	4m	Cost per ad
Sittercity.com	USA only	1.9m	Cost per ad
Aupair-world.net	DE	500k	€39 for 3 mts
GreatAuPair.com	USA	280k	$175 6 mts/ $120 3 mts / $60 1 mt
Gonannies.com	USA	120k	$49 -40 days/ $79-90 days/ $149 -1 year
Easyaupair.com	UK	93k	£31.99 3 mts, £55.99 6 mts £89.99 12 mts

*(Source: Google Ad Planner)

Advantages and disadvantages of the competitors' offerings

Advantages – the main competitors have huge volumes of traffic with an extensive database of care providers to easily match the needs of the care seeker. It's likely the care seeker will find solutions very quickly.

Disadvantages – some of the sites are trying to provide too many services so some of the information tends to get lost on the site. Offering too many services may restrict the ability to engage in niche marketing, and specific niche SEO strategies.

5 Internal Marketing Audit

The internal marketing audit focuses on the activities and performance of your company within your internal marketing environment. It should cover an evaluation of the following four sections, where applicable, and you have information available:

Operating Results

This covers operating results (by product, customer, and geographic region) for sales, market share, profit margins and costs.

Strategic Issues Analysis

The strategic issues analysis will typically answer the following questions;

- What are our current marketing objectives?
- How do we currently segment the market?
- What is our competitive advantage (if any)?
- What are our core competencies?
- How our products are positioned in the market place?
- How are our products placed in terms of market attractiveness and company strength?

Marketing Mix Effectiveness

Each element of the marketing mix (product, promotion, price and place) is evaluated.

Marketing Structures and Systems

The marketing structures and systems of your company are evaluated to identify what exists and its effectiveness. These may include your marketing organization, marketing training, and intra and interdepartmental communication. Marketing systems include marketing information systems, the marketing planning system and the marketing control systems.

If you don't have any marketing systems already, you will need to identify how you will introduce the appropriate marketing systems and controls to effectively monitor your marketing activities.

Childcare.com Sample

As Childcare.com is a startup company, there is no previous operating experience to report on. The following sections summarize the internal marketing environment.

Marketing Objectives

Our marketing objectives are to;

- effectively engage with our target customer to reinforce the Childcare.com service offering. We will do this on a regular basis, mainly via our email marketing campaign.

- promote our service at every opportunity to gain constant recognition. We will actively promote our business online through our social media activities, to build our brand awareness and positively enforce our online profile.

- continually communicate with our customers in a friendly/no-nonsense manner. We will take advantage of every opportunity to communicate directly with our customer.

Market Segmentation

Our market can be segmented into the following broad segments.

- Families/ legal guardians seeking childcare
- Chilldcare providers
- Business promoters

Core Competencies

We are a startup organization with the following core competencies;

- In house development/ IT skills – all website development is undertaken internally
- Digital media experience
- Project management experience
- Operations management experience
- Dedicated, full-time staff working on Childcare.com

Training Needs Identified

We will focus on Facebook social networking to boost awareness of our service offering. Given our limited knowledge in this area we will need to enhance our Facebook skills to fully tap into the power of Facebook. We have identified two online training resources that will help us to develop our Facebook skills: **Facebook Influence** (http://tinyurl.com/6s6queu) and **Facebook Training for Business** (http://tinyurl.com/7bomqa8).

Service Positioning

Initially, it is expected that our service can be categorized with low market share and low growth. In the early phase, the new service is likely to absorb huge amounts of time until the digital media and marketing efforts bear fruit. The plan is to move the service offering to a good position within a high growth market, thus generating high income.

6 SWOT Analysis

A SWOT analysis is a structured approach to evaluating the strategic position of your business by identifying your strengths, weaknesses, opportunities and threats.

It provides a simple method of synthesizing the results of the marketing audit by summarizing your company's strengths and weaknesses as they relate to the external opportunities and threats.

Strengths and weaknesses will typically derive from your internal marketing audit analysis.

Opportunities and threats will typically derive from your external marketing audit analysis.

A good way to present your SWOT results is in a table. See the Childcare.com example below.

Childcare.com SWOT

STRENGHTS	WEAKNESSES
➢ Organization skills	➢ New to market
➢ IT technical skills	➢ Limited resources
➢ Digital Marketing Experience	➢ Limited marketing budget
➢ Dedicated management team	➢ Training needed for advanced social media networking
➢ Support from family and friends	
OPPORTUNITIES	**THREATS**
➢ Scalable technology to easily deploy new features quickly	➢ No barriers to entry
➢ Potential to add new services and revenue streams	➢ Recession – families out of work may no longer require carers
	➢ Free online networking and job sites

7 Assumptions

It's important to keep a note of the key assumptions you make as you are developing each section of your marketing plan.

Childcare.com Sample

The key assumptions for delivering this marketing plan are;

- Revenue from sales will fund a Google Adwords campaign. We will invest revenue back into the business to promote our website through pay per click advertising.
- The Childcare.com service offering will stimulate word of mouth referrals.
- Families will continue to require childcare services and be comfortable recruiting care givers online.
- Revenue from sales will fund recruitment of digital marketing experts.

8 Marketing Objectives

Once you have completed your marketing audit and SWOT analysis, you can then set relevant marketing objectives for your company. There are generally two types of objectives that you need to consider: strategic thrust and strategic objectives.

Strategic Thrust

Strategic thrust defines which products you want to sell in which markets. The main options are:

- existing products in existing markets (market penetration or expansion)
- new/related products for existing markets (product development)
- existing products in new/related markets (market development)
- new/related products in new/related markets (entry into new markets)

Strategic Objectives

Strategic objectives for your products and services need to be set. The options are to build sales and market share, hold, harvest (improve profit margins) and divest (drop or sell product).

A table is a good way to present this information. In the Childcare.com example, a table maybe used to highlight the market size for each target market, and the target share expected. Adopting this approach will also give you an estimate of the sales volumes expected. It is important to state a time period by when you expect to achieve your sales volumes.

For example, assuming there are 20,000 child minders in London (UK), and Childcare.com expects 4%, or 800 child minders, to advertize. If they charge $10 per child minder, the expected sales revenue is $8000 for this target customer. You could complete a similar table for each of your target countries and/or major target cities within each country.

Childcare.com Sample

Strategic Thrust

Market Penetration and Expansion

Childcare.com will initially launch with the service for care seekers (families) to recruit care providers (au pairs, nannies, childminders) directly. Research has shown that online recruiting for care staff is accepted within our target countries. The marketing strategy is to penetrate the market and gradually gain market share by effectively implementing an expansion plan.

Service Development

Subsequent phases of our website will incorporate other services and revenue streams. With each new release we will look to expand our service within existing and new markets.

Market Development

The technology platform, and business model processes, will be rolled out to other relevant online services such as senior care.

Strategic Objectives

Market Share

The key strategic objective is to build sales and market share.

The following table outlines the market size for each of our target markets, and the revenue volumes, by each target customer we expect to achieve by the end of 2015. (_Note_: _for this example, only the first line of the table is completed._)

Target	Post Job Ad		Child minders		Business Advertisers	
	Est.	Target Share	Est.	Target Share	Est.	Target Share
London	10,000	5%	20,000	4%	5,000	5%

Keep it simple

Our objective for product and service development is to keep it simple. Develop simple, easy to use solutions that the market want, and have them available when the customer wants to use them.

9 Core Strategy

Core marketing strategy involves the achievement of marketing objectives through the determination of target markets, the setting of competitor targets and the creation of a competitive advantage.

Target Markets

You need to decide which target market (s) you will offer your products and/or services to. A target market can be defined as a group of consumers/ organizations (segment) that your company wishes to aim its offering and communications at.

It defines **WHERE** your company wishes to compete.

Competitor Targets

Besides targeting consumers/organizations, your company will also need to choose competitor targets. Weak competitors may be viewed as easy prey and resource channeled to attach them. The choice of target market may define your competitor targets, which in turn will influence your marketing strategy. For example, market segments with weak competitors may be attractive targets.

Competitor Advantage

A competitive advantage is a clear performance differential over competitors on factors that are important to your target consumers/organizations.

This provides the basis of **HOW** your company competes.

Major success is dependent on your company creating a competitive advantage by being better, being faster at anticipating or responding better to customer needs than your competitors, or being closer to establishing close long-term relationships with your customers.

Childcare.com Sample

Target Markets

The target customer segments are families/guardians, child minders, business promoters and care workers. Initially marketing efforts will focus on the childcare market in the UK, followed by the USA and Australia.

Competitor Targets

The main competitor targets are;

- Online Agencies
- Free Online Advertising Sites
- Traditional Agencies

Competitive Advantage

Childcare.com addresses the need for finding information on childcare solutions.

Unique Selling Point (USP)

Our unique selling point will focus on how Childcare.com is here to help families find childcare that meets their needs. Childcare.com takes the pain out of recruiting.

Benefits of Childcare.com

Value for money - cheaper than using a traditional agency.

10 Marketing Mix

By defining your target market and understanding the needs of your target consumers/organizations, you are in a good position to create a marketing mix to meet those needs better than your competition. Decisions have to be made regarding product, promotion, price and place, which are the building blocks for your marketing mix.

Product

Product (and/or service) decisions involve choices around brand names, features, quality and design, packaging, warranties, and the services that will accompany the product offering.

Promotion

Promotion decisions involve choices on how you are going to promote your product/service to your target market. You will need to make decisions on advertizing, personal selling, direct and indirect marketing, sales and promotions, as well as public relations.

Price

Pricing decisions involve choices on how much you are going to charge for your product/service. Decisions on your list price, discounts, credit terms and payment periods have to be made. You'll need to carefully review your competitor pricing before you set your own prices.

Place

Place decisions involve choices on how you are going to distribute your product/service. What distribution channels are you going to use and how will you manage these? If you need a physical presence then the location of outlets is important. Decisions on your methods of transportation and inventory levels must be made if you are selling a product.

Childcare.com Sample

Childcare.com is an online services business so some of the above marketing mix does not apply. When compiling your own marketing mix, you need to pick out all the areas that are relevant to your company.

Service Offering (Product)

The Childcare.com service offering is to connect care givers and care seekers online in a fast and efficient way. Some of the main characteristics of our service are;

- Simple, easy to navigate website
- Simple tools to help our customer effectively find solutions to their needs
- No-nonsense straightforward terms of engagement
- No hidden costs

Guarantees

We offer a money back guarantee if no job applications are received within 5 days.

Customer Service

We strive to provide excellent customer service through online self-help guides, email and by telephone.

Service Positioning / Branding

Communication with our customer will be personalized and friendly. Our brand is all about going back to basics;

- Great value
- Excellent customer service
- Straightforward and easy to use website

We will deliver what our customer wants. In particular, our brand identity traits are;

- Honesty
- Innovative
- Simple
- Easy
- Friendly
- Clear

Our tone of voice is that 'we are here to help' facilitating people to make a difference in their lives.

Price

The table below outlines our main services an price for each.

	Retail Price
Service A – post a job	$10
Service B - childminder profile	$10

All payments will be processed online, using a secure payment gateway.

Place

Childare.com is an online service and all interaction with our customer base is online.

Promotion

A combination of Push and Pull marketing activities will be exercised to promote Childcare.com.

Push strategies to include Search Engine Optimization (SEO), Social Media (Facebook, Twitter, YouTube, blogging etc), Networking and trade shows.

Pull strategies to include online registration form, loyalty discounts for returning customers and their friends, forum community engagement

Digital Marketing

Search Engine Optimization (SEO) techniques will be used to get Childcare.com recognised more frequently when people perform searches on sites such as Google or Yahoo. The objective is to increase SEO rankings so that Childcare.com gets seen by more people.

The following strategies will be adopted to increase SEO rankings.

Keywords

A selection of keywords commonly used in searches for care givers will be targeted on Childcare.com, blogs and backlink posts. The objective being to get organic listings on the first page of Google for these search terms. The keywords will be also be used for the Childcare.com website title, description and keywords in the META tags.

Inbound links (backlinks)

A strategy of increasing inbound links to Childcare.com will be rigorously pursued. Initially, Childcare.com will be registered on free business directory sites and on free job listing sites. We will purchase a directory submissions tool (http://tinyurl.com/82e568p) to help us automate and manage the directory submission process.

Local search listings

Childcare.com will be registered on local sites within each target area. Active jobs will be posted to local job search sites and local listings, such as craigslist to attract care providers.

Email Marketing / Ezine

Initially we plan to use the free version of Get Response (http://tinyurl.com/7qe4t3n) for managing and growing our email marketing list. We will utilize the tools within Get Response to manage the distribution of a monthly Ezine.

Paid Advertising

Google Adwords and Facebook will be the main paid advertising campaigns adopted. Our strategy is to find good volume, low value pay-per-click key words for these campaigns.

Social Media

Our social media strategy is to become involved in conversations relevant to our service offering, for example, topics on au pairs, childcare. Our social media goal is to develop our brand, expand our customer base, to educate and entertain our target customers.

- Blog

  Our blog will actively promote the services offered by Childcare.com. Our blog will be used to build up our reputation, as well as direct traffic to Childcare.com. Our blog will post keyword rich content. Our objective is to post a consistent and relevant blog at least once a week. We will use Site Build as the software to host and promote our blog (http://tinyurl.com/7u225m6)

- Face Book

Our Facebook page will be used post information on service offerings, promotions and latest jobs.

- Twitter

We will actively follow our target customer base with the objectives of gathering information on our customers, and engaging in conversations relevant to our service offering.

Article Marketing

We will actively engage in article marketing with the objective of building our reputation, as well as directing traffic to Childcare.com using our selected keywords. Some popular article sites we will work with are Ezinearticles and goarticles.

To save time on the article submission process, we will purchase **Article Submitter,** (http://tinyurl.com/756thy3) an inexpensive product, to assist us with some of the article submission and management tasks.

Video Marketing

Our channel on youtube will post videos relevant to our service offering.

Our Flickr account will be used to upload images and videos promoting our service offering with our selected keywords.

Loyalty discounts

Paid advertisers on Childcare.com qualify for regular discounts on further service offerings.

Referrals and word of mouth

Registered members on Childcare.com qualify for regular discount promotions for their family and friends.

Offline Advertising

Childcare.com will be displayed on all off-line marketing activity, such as business cards, brochures/flyers, direct mail, invoices, advertisements, PR releases and gifts.

Conversion Strategy

The objective of our conversion strategy is to increase sales conversions online by reducing customer anxiety.

The key elements of this strategy are;

- **Professional website**

Childcare.com is a professional, simple and easy to use website. Our secure payments facility is a reputable online merchant.

- **Privacy Policy**

A clear privacy policy statement will be readily available.

- **Logos and links**

The Childcare.com logo is easy to distinguish and will be clearly visible on all page views. Links to other pages on Childcare.com and recommended websites will be other professional websites.

- **Testimonials**

Trust is a big factor when recruiting childcare providers. Customer testimonials will be clearly visible on Childcare.com.

- **Guarantees**

Our money back guarantee will be clearly visible and followed through with in a consistent manner.

11 Organization and Implementation

Your marketing plan needs a marketing organization, or assigned resources, to implement it and a budget to make it happen. Reorganization may mean the establishment of a new marketing structure or the creation of a marketing department for the first time. Consideration should also be given to implementation issues, and how you plan to overcome these.

Your implementation plan will focus on **WHO** is responsible for various activities, **HOW** the strategy should be carried out, **WHERE** things will happen, and **WHEN** action will take place. They all need to be clearly identified and documented, along with the assumptions you make.

In our sample plan, Childcare.com is a small startup with limited resources.

Childcare.com Sample

As the main marketing activities are predominantly focused online, digital marketing experts will be employed to build up our marketing team.

Year 1
Two digital marketing specialists hired with responsibility for targeting the UK.
Year 2
Three further digital marketing specialists hired with responsibility for targeting the USA and Australia

Their main responsibilities are in the areas of driving traffic to Childcare.com, and to achieve the conversion targets for their specific country.

Budget

Resource Procurement

- Five digital marketing @ annual salary $45k

Paid Advertising campaign

- Year 1 - $50,000
- Year 2 - $50,000
- Year 3 - $65,000
- Year 4 - $84,000

Assumptions: revenue from sales will be used to fund paid advertising and staff salaries.

Implementation Plan

The following project management work breakdown structure outlines the main areas of work for the initial implementation of this marketing plan. A detailed marketing implementation plan will be developed, and responsibilities, and targets, assigned to the team.

For the moment we are a small startup, and Mary is the only full-time member of the marketing team assigned tasks.

To overcome our limited resource challenge, we will look to outsource and/or automate as much of the standard processes as we can.

Work Area	Description	Assigned to	Due Date
Social media	Setup the main social media accounts – FB, twitter, Youtube, blog, and document the social media timetable and objectives for each medium (i.e. blog post at least once a week)	Mary	Oct 2011
Keyword	Identify and document key word strategy	Mary	Oct 2011
Back links	Register Childcare.com on business directories and start the back link building campaign using keywords	Mary	Nov 2011
Free job posting sites	Start to build up a list of free job posting sites for attracting candidates	Mary	Nov 2011
Promotion	Start to build up a list of UK sites for promotion	Mary	Nov 2011
Business Advertisers package	Document a package for business advertisers – costs, benefits, site statistics	Mary	Nov 2011
Hiring Plan	Define job descriptions, responsibilities and targets for marketing staff	Mary	Dec 2011

Automation

As a small start-up company, with limited resources and time, we plan to utilize as many free and reasonably priced Search Engine Optimization tools to speed up our online marketing efforts. At this stage we have identified the following tools as being very beneficial for maximizing our digital marketing effort.

Magic Submitter - http://tinyurl.com/756thy3
This software will automatically generate backlinks to Chldcare.com

Directory Submitter – http://tinyurl.com/82e568p
This tool will automate some of the directory submission process for us, as well as saving us a huge amount of time trying to find free directory sites on the web.

Backlinkutopia - http://tinyurl.com/73679t7
This tool will also assist in automating our digital marketing activities.

12 Control

The aim of our control systems is to evaluate the results of our marketing plan so that corrective action can be taken if performance does not match objectives. Google analytics will be the main tool used to constantly monitor site visits, to understand the effectiveness of our keyword strategy and targeted backlinks campaign. Subsequent information will be gathered from Alexa.com.

The main metrics we will use to monitor our ongoing performance are;

Traffic – On a daily/weekly basis we will track visitors to the site, referring websites, and locations to ascertain if this is in-line with visitor expectations. Adjust accordingly if results are not achieved.

Key word analysis – on a weekly/monthly basis a review of the key word strategy to ascertain the site position on Google for each target key word will be conducted and assessed.

Conversion rates – on a daily/weekly/monthly basis keep track of the sales conversion rate. Look for corrective action if sales targets are not met.

Customer feedback – actively request and monitor customer feedback. Work with developer to implement customer enhancing changes.

Social media timetable – actively monitor social media deliverables against strategy. For example, is the blog updated once a week with relevant content?

Google page rank – the Google toolbar (http://toolbar.google.com) will show the Childcare.com page rank, along with all competitor sites.

System uptime – objective is 99.9% uptime, 24/7, 365 days a year.

13 Useful Tools And Resources

Confirming Sufficient Market Size

Compete (www.compete.com), Quantcast (www.quantcast.com), Alexa (www.alexa.com) and the Google Ad Planner (www.google.com/adplanner/) are good tools for finding the number of monthly visitors for most popular websites, in addition to the search terms that generate the most traffic for them. Spyfu (www.spyfu.com) – download competitors' online advertising spending, keywords and adwords details.

Keyword Search Tools

Keywords are the words or phrases people use when they search for something on the web. For instance, if someone is looking for a website selling 'baby monitors' they will probably enter 'baby monitor' into the search engine's search box.

You will need to find the keywords or phrases people use to search for the products and services you offer. Then make sure that you add your keywords and phrases into the directories when you are adding your site to the directory listing.

Some keyword tools are;
- The Google Search Tool
     (https://adwords.google.com/select/**KeywordTool**External)
- SEOBook Keyword Tool - (http://tools.seobook.com)
- Web Ferret – www.webferret.com

Domain Registration

- **Hostgator** - http://bit.ly/w66EtA

- **Namecheap** - http://bit.ly/yisSc5

Blog or Build a Website

- Site Build - http://bit.ly/zJ6t7F

- Wordpress – www.wordpress.com

- Blogger – www.blogger.com

ABOUT THE AUTHOR

P A Flanagan, BBS, MPM, is an online business owner, business writer and entrepreneur. The author has over twenty years industry experience and is now bringing this experience to a series of How to Guides. These business writing guides will help you to write your own business documents by following the easy steps and business examples within the guides.

www.ingramcontent.com/pod-product-compliance
Lightning Source LLC
Chambersburg PA
CBHW080622200526
45166CB00028B/1528